EGONOMICS 101

The Awakening Has Begun...
Within...
or Without You

TOMMY JOE LAUX

Egonomics 101
Copyright © 2023 by Tommy Joe Laux

Published in the United States of America
ISBN   Paperback: 979-8-89091-213-8
ISBN   eBook: 979-8-89091-214-5

All rights reserved. No part of this publication may be reproduced, stored in a retrieval system or transmitted in any way by any means, electronic, mechanical, photocopy, recording or otherwise without the prior permission of the author except as provided by USA copyright law.

The opinions expressed by the author are not necessarily those of ReadersMagnet, LLC.

ReadersMagnet, LLC
10620 Treena Street, Suite 230
San Diego, California, 92131 USA
1.619. 354. 2643 | www.readersmagnet.com

Cover design by Tifanny Curaza
Interior design by Don De Guzman

Contents

Dedication v
Acknowledgments vii
Introduction..viii

Chapter 1: My Near-Death Experience 1
Chapter 2: The Message......................................7
Chapter 3: Good Versus Evil 13
Chapter 4: The Return Of Jesus?
How Can Someone Return,
That Has Never Left? 18
Chapter 5: The Human Race? What's
The Hurry? 23
Chapter 6: Why?..28
Chapter 7: Dreams..35

Conclusion..47

DEDICATION

My Lovely Family

From the left is Tommy Laux, Alicea Laux, Julie Laux, and Raymond Laux. Family Photo Taken 2007

Egonomics 101 is dedicated to the spirit of all humanity—past, present, and future.

Mainly to my wife, Julie Renee Laux, and our son, Raymond Garrett Laux, may they rest in peace.

To our daughter, Alicea Nichole Laux Thompson, thank you for the unconditional love and support throughout your existence. I love you more than you can imagine.

To all of my family, friends, and associates, thank you for trying to understand this unexplainable journey. This includes those of us who are programmed to deny the existence of anything that we can't experience and explain with our common five senses.

Arlo Bybee 2021

My 3 years old one and only Grandson from my daughter Alicea Laux, and Andrew Bybee.

ACKNOWLEDGMENTS

First and foremost, I want to thank God for my life, death, and rebirth into this experience.

To all of my family, friends, and associates, thank you for trying to understand this unexplainable journey.

To Dr. Vicky Thomas, DCH, for the hypnotherapy and input with chapter 7 regarding "Dreams."

To Paul and Collette Pondella Shadowland Foundation.

To Joey Fulco and his amazingly talented family band of musicians; the love is obvious!

To Livia Martinez at Stratton Press. My cheerleader, for pushing me to the finish line.

And of course, Ann McIndoo, my author's coach, who got this book out of my head and into my hands.

INTRODUCTION

2016 Tommy

With His Best Friend Moonshine and the 1954 Chevy panel truck that the *Shifter* was made for.

This is my testimony of what I, or should we say, my soul, experienced from my own death. The first thing that comes to mind is that life is energy, and death is that energy transformed into a greater energy or the universe.

What I saw is impossible to put into words so that everyone will understand, but I will do my best. What we experience or what I experienced in that moment was like my soul being removed from the human form or human condition. My spirit/soul was more alive than ever. It left the confining container of my body. I was again rejoined with the Great Spirit, God, the Universe, or whatever labels we humans want to call it. We get so hung up on the literal words that we lose the meanings.

Anyway, what died at that moment, along with the body, was my ego. Before that moment, I didn't even know I had an ego, but sure as hell, there it was, decomposing with my container. My soul/spirit was free of all negativity for that brief moment. I was returned to the energy of love that I was before I was born.

Like I said, it's hard to put into words something that most of us don't get to return from. I was shown not only my past fifty years of this life; what I saw was many past lives, present moment, and future. More accurately, the future was just a projection of what will be if we keep doing the same bullshit. The whole human species has been playing the same game for many thousands of years.

The power trip. The dark ages never end. If we keep our collective heads in the sand, so to speak. I say collective because every one of us is in this bubble together. We all have these same gifts to some degree. The gifts I am speaking of are soul and ego, positive and negative, light and dark.

We are born into this beautiful world as pure love or soul. Babies have no ego. No negative, no hate. They learn that from the system. The Ego-system. We humans have been under this same system for many thousands of years, for so long that we call it human nature. It's not!

There is nothing natural about greed. Yes, it is very common among us well-trained humans, but it's not nature. We need to move on to the new age of awareness. We need to all become aware of our own truth and our own lies. We all have to share our gifts of enlightenment.

We have been programmed by this human Ego-system! To quote Eckhart Tolle, "The ego wants to want, more than it wants to have. And the Ego will never, ever, become satisfied."

Whether individual or collective, it's all the same system or the same type of system. The computers that we use today are modeled after the human brain. Basically, they are designed to make it easier for us to learn the rules of man or our controllers. This human ego-system has been supported by the most brilliant minds that ever lived and ever died. This ego-system is clearly self-serving and designed to work in compliance within and without the human form. We are creating and becoming the parts of this high-tech machine. Without a doubt, we have created a mechanical monster.

To me, the monster or demon is so easy to see, even the one that I hold dear to me and very near to me. It is my brain. It's not bad or evil; however, it is only controlled by my spirits and me. Not yours and not theirs, whoever they are. Whenever I allow my brain or my controller to be tricked into submission, to be controlled by any force outside of my body, that is when I am, or I become, just another part of the machine.

We tend to do this more often than we are aware of. Most of us, anyway. That is why awareness is so important. And so rare, by God's standards. To be totally honest, before my accident and subsequent awakening, I had no idea that I was not awake and aware. This makes it easy for me now to understand the resistance of the masses to want to awaken.

If you spent your whole life learning or training how to control the masses, then the last thing your ego or your trainer wants to happen is for the masses to control itself. So it will find ways to make itself needed, even if that means self-sabotage.

TOMMY JOE LAUX

The Ego Claw Shifter

I carved this claw out of purple heart wood and formed it around a stone ball made of Jasper from Madagascar. I made this for the shifter knob in my classic restored 1954 Chevy Panel Truck. After it was finished and installed, it dawned on me how it relates to my book as the tight grip that the human Ego condition has on the world.

This is one of those ways that our Spirit and God speak through our subconscious art of self-expression. When I created the shifter knob, I was not thinking about the book. I just wanted to see if I could make a ball and claw, like a table leg, only small enough to fit in my hand. Like the rest of the panel truck it boosts my ego, or self-esteem. Hence the ego claw shifter. There are many other personal features in that panel truck that make it one of a kind. The headliner in the back, is a quilt made by my wife Julie Laux, using 9 of my old T-shirts from band gigs and motorcycle runs, along with old levies and bandanas.

Tying it all together, the shift in consciousness, both personal and collective, that we human beings are here to experience, is to learn to be honest with ourselves and each other.

Tommy 1999

My first Tattoo: Smile 'N' Fish, Band Logo.

CHAPTER ONE

My Near-Death Experience

In 2008, I was a happy and content man, with a beautiful soul partner, my wife, Julie Renee Laux, and two beautiful and respectable children, Alicea Nicole Laux Thompson and Raymond Garrett Laux. I was the president of a very successful company called TLC Woodworks, Inc., and the cofounder of an original music band called the Smile 'N' Fish band. Life was and still is as good as it gets.

On July 20, 2008, my wife and I were on our way home from a family reunion held at my sister's house in Pueblo, Colorado. We were about a half hour away from her best friend's house and our first leg of the trip home. We were on my 2007 Harley Davidson (Road King) motorcycle. Like I said earlier, life was as good as it gets.

The Accident

As we were cruising down the highway, outside of Montrose, Colorado, an old couple in a Chevy pickup truck made a left in front of us and we crashed. My wife was pronounced dead either at the scene or at the first hospital in Montrose, and I was airlifted to Saint Mary's Hospital in Grand Junction in critical condition, where I was in a coma for about four days.

In that one event, I flat-lined three times. I was in bad shape and not expected to live by the medical staff. This is from my out-of-body consciousness or my soul's perspective: I was in another higher dimension of consciousness.

It is so hard to put into the words what was shown to me. After all, how does a carpenter, an Outlaw Carpenter(s) (the name of my new business), begin to explain how he was shown a glimpse of eternity and infinity and, yes, even death? My own death, and also my soul mate's death, or should I say, transformation of consciousness and awareness.

Anyway, I was committed to come back to this dimension or this reality to try as I may, to share and help anyone who wants and/or needs to know more about the failure of our system, the ego-system that has been in place for the thousands of years. It is obvious to all human beings that the system cannot and will not fix itself. By default, the ego in all of us, including mine, would rather not be exposed!

However, mine was brought into the light at death and sent back to this reality to share.

Please don't get me wrong, I did not come back to save the world or the planet or even the people; that's not my purpose for coming back to this reality. My purpose is clearly to spread as much love and truth as humanly possible and as spiritually possible. Again, don't get me wrong. This is not a new religion or a new political platform or even a utopian dream. What it is, is an attempt at helping to raise the consciousness of humanity, even if I only reach a few precious souls, I will remain grateful for the opportunity.

As I began writing this book and talking about it probably about five or six years ago, 2010 or so, I literally had to get past my own ego and listen to my soul or spirit. While recalling the experience and talking to friends and family about it, several people had asked me if I have read Eckhart Tolle's books. I had not even heard of him.

Then something amazing happened. I went to a friend's house to tell him about something I had written that morning. He gave me a borrowed copy of A New Earth. That was cool, but the amazing part was when I got home, the TV was on an old Oprah Winfrey show from about 2007 with her interviewing Eckhart Tolle about A New Earth. My girlfriend at the time was excited that I got home at just the right time to catch it. After watching the show, I said, "I feel like I have already read this book," but I knew I had not. I didn't read much back then. However, after reading that book, I was amazed how similar the message is. I was not overeducated; I didn't even graduate high school. Therefore, I didn't think it was possible or my trained ego didn't think it was possible to help even myself, let alone anyone else.

Fortunately for me, I was shown how easy it is to communicate with the other side, and I learned this from the other side or, rather, another higher dimension. Keep in mind and in heart, that most people can only teach people what people taught them. That is where the human ego comes into play.

What my soul experienced from the higher dimension, and this is without my ego, as it was dying along with my body, is that the greatest struggle of every human being alive is between their own ears. What I am talking about is the battle of the soul-self and the ego-self.

To describe that dimension to others who have not been there yet? That would be like describing a world where everyone is free, where there is no better or worse. Where everyone knows what everyone knows. There is no need for deception or lies. Because without the human conditioned ego, there is no fear, no struggle, no battle, no judgment, no secrets, no worries.

For me to describe that dimension in physical terms would be misleading because, as humans, we are creating that dimension for ourselves, by our actions and beliefs here and now! So be good, not God.

The way this was shown to me in the other dimension was very simple and without words. Without thought, without ego, and its logical defense mechanism. To put it simply is to say it was pure and free energy. Positive energy was all my soul could feel or should I say, accept, in that dimension.

And I am feeling that right now as I write this. As I recall this experience, it takes me back to that peaceful place and timeless time. Out of my mind? Yes, of course, and out of my body also. I go there often when I am alone and am allowed to go deep into myself. You can call it meditation or prayer or whatever you like.

When I say, "Into myself," it is what projects me out there into the essence of the source of life. What I mean is to say I can see my human ego form, struggling with my formless soul, trying to bring it back into shape and into this reality. The ego is taught to fear its own death.

On a subconscious level, I believe we all know this. It has always fascinated me, when I hear experts say that we only use, more or less, 10 percent of our brain. That statement didn't make sense to me. My question was, why is that? And what is the other 90 percent there for? The answer to that question was somewhat shocking to me. That is where the subconscious genetic memory is stored. The Pandora's Box or the genie in the bottle.

It is where all deeds are stored, the good, the bad, and the ugly. The history of your parents, grandparents, great-grandparents, and so on. It is a great big bag of mixed emotions. The ancient wisdoms are there, along with the fear of prediction. I was shown the reason for suppressed memory. The brain automatically deletes traumatic experience to some degree. Survival of the ego depends on this.

The way this was revealed to me as positive (SOUL) and negative (EGO) and in this realm or this existence, balance and acceptance is essential. And that balance is only attainable with honest awareness of both energies that we all have access to. To say that I am here because I think, as in, "I think, therefore I am," is only true from the human egotistic point of view.

Now let's spin that famous quote around and say, "I am, therefore I think." It's still the ego in me trying to be clever. And now from the soul, or spirit, in me: "I feel, therefore I am." That feeling is great. That's not to say that I am great because I am only one part of this whole human experience. You will rarely hear me say that I feel your pain because I don't. I would rather say: "I feel you. I feel your spirit, your essence."

CHAPTER TWO

THE MESSAGE

What was shown to me from that other dimension is honestly nothing new. This message of another world, another existence, a better world, this message has been here all along. However, most of us are inadvertently conditioned to fear at an early age. We are, as human beings, conditioned to believe in the human condition. Everything has been said so to speak. "Pay no attention to the man behind the curtain."

Anyway, back to the message that I for one, along with countless others, have been sent back here to share, which is the direct awareness of the powers that be. Both human and non-human, both seen and unseen, both conscious and unconscious, both history and mystery. My story is a mystery, and this book is by all means, part of this revolution of consciousness. I mean, evolution of consciousness.

I am and always have been a doubting Thomas, according to my wife, anyway. That is probably, and most likely, the reason why I found myself hard to train. I was, for the first fifty years of my life, a hardworking and subconscious machine. I questioned everything and understood nothing.

I was content with all the ups and downs of life as a self-taught happy idiot. I did not know how to compete. I did learn to survive and be happy with whatever comes my way and let it go if I could or I should. In retrospect, I felt no gratification in conforming to the norm.

I learned early in life the rule: lead, follow, or get out of the way. So the easiest way in my opinion, or the path of least resistance, logically, was to get out of the way! So I became a carpenter. I became a master craftsman and passionate about bringing some of the otherwise dead trees back to life, sort of.

As far as I knew, I was not competing with anyone else but myself. I was not retarded, just challenged.

What I mean to say is, I constantly challenged myself. I could not understand what they meant when they said to think outside the box. I must have ditched school on that day. So lucky for me, I didn't get a box, at least not a strong box. At this point in my life, in my opinion, that proverbial box is the human ego.

For that matter, in human form anyway, that box could be labeled spirit. Or soul, the label doesn't matter. What matters is it's still a box! Or should I say, it's still a container. And in that container is you. Every thought, every emotion, every experience, every dream, every nightmare, every blessing, and every curse. And after all is said and done, you are the judge, jury, and executioner of your own committee or self.

All of this is mindless babble or wishful thinking to the trained eyes of the ego-system. However, trained or untrained makes no difference to the powers that be. The human powers that be, and this includes both church and state, have one goal in common. And that is control. Mind control, that is.

The driving force is fear, hate, envy, and any and all negative actions and reactions is what fuel this machine. That is what fuels the ego-system, which is, by divine design, eating itself or trying to kill itself from the inside out. The ego is the keeper of the box, vessel, the arc of the covenant, whatever we think has the power.

In other words, we think it is the thinker, the brain, the mind. "Are you out of your mind?" How many times have we all heard that? Or more importantly, as adults, we constantly ask ourselves, "WTF was I thinking? I must have been out of my mind. Oh well, I fucked up, I trusted you!" And this is all in my head, so to speak. Between my ego (lower self) and my soul or spirit (higher self).

Now at this day and age, multiply that by over seven billion people, and most of us are trained to fear the unknown, fear the ego, fear the illusion of fear. We worship freedom and condemn it in others at the exact same time. Hence, the happy idiot that I claim to be at times, or appear to be, goes unnoticed. Kind of crazy, isn't it?

I am neither high class nor low class. I no longer worry. I no longer worry about anything. Life and/or death, it's all the same to me. It is real and surreal at the same time. I am truthfully and thankfully living the dream. And I no longer have to worry about who loves or who hates and who's fucking who no longer concerns me. As long as I'm not fucking myself unknowingly.

I have unwittingly surrendered my overprotective ego. This means yes, I am out of my mind, only when and if necessary. And this is by choice now. It feels good to be free of the conditioners of fear. Just recently, I attempted to express or share this reality with a few close friends that I consider relatively aware and awake.

Yet they were dead set and sure that fear is absolutely necessary for the survival of the tribe and/or self. I said fear is a wasted negative emotion. To me, fear is the ego's reaction to whatever alarms you. I tried to explain the difference between awareness and fear, with no avail. So I conceded and thanked my spirits for the un-conditioning of my soul.

The reason for this book and the message is to help all classes of human beings. Mainly, though, I was sent back to help myself first. To learn from and then teach my little people, my two children, Alicea and Raymond. They are, after all, a reflection of their mother and me, and of course, the social engineers of society, as we know it. This brings a tear to my eye. Not because I failed to reach my son before he died, but because I did.

As difficult as this is to understand, it is as difficult to explain. So fuck it, here it is: We are not alone in this world. We are not the most intelligent beings on this plain or any other plain of existence.

In other words, believe it or not, humans are not that smart. We just think we are. Some of us do, anyway.

We think with fear, or should I say, most are afraid to think we are trained by the machine, to believe in the machine. To consume and obey and then throw away. Thou shalt not question the gods of government. They have the authority to create and destroy. And they do.

When I say gods of government, I am not referring to the left or the right. I am not referring to the north or the south. In this reality, in this life, in this world, "The Truth within You Lies." That is a song written by a great unknown artist and friend of mine, Michael Vernetti. He was also a member of my band Smile 'N' Fish for a while.

The Truth within You Lies

Every time you look away from me
Every time you see just what you see And every time
I see it in your eyes
It's clear to see the truth within your lies

The path you take that leads away from here
The laugh you fake when you've been drinking beer
The tears that drown the silence of your cries
Can't help but hide the truth within your lies

Fears of when our eyes will meet again
Mirrors that show you who is lost within
Push on the walls, open the door

EGONOMICS 101

Answer the calls, silence the roar
Keep on holding on is what she tries
Surrounded by the truth within her ties

I walk with you, but you are all alone
I want to show you what you haven't known
I led you to that place of open skies
You turned and saw the truth within your lies

You understand, but you cannot comprehend
You must return what you really meant to send
Give everything you've got to realize
Sometimes all the truth within your lies

The beast before us echoed into flight
Released before we sheltered for the night
Somewhere, somehow, someday, you will arise
And turn and find the truth within your lies

Now, depending on how you read that or how you feel about the words and the world for that matter is dependent on you or, rather, your human condition of ego and soul.

CHAPTER THREE

Good versus Evil

At the risk of sounding redundant, I have to keep reminding myself that I am, as well as you, only one small part of this infinite experience. "Do as I say and not as I do." I can't be the only one who has heard that before.

For the love of God, did you read the Good Book? I have been asked that question over and over and the answer is no. I have not. But I have heard a lot about it. And…and …and…I saw the movie Oh, God! and the cartoons. I went to school as required by law, and I failed to graduate. I got a lot of Fs in life, fucking-A, that could be why I say fuck a lot. I don't know, it's just a hunch.

Good is God with an extra O, right? Evil is Devil with a dropped D. Plus or minus is on every plan, every blue print. Yes, even the Master Plan of the human beings. Positive and negative energy is constantly fluctuating and pulsing around us at all times. Inside and outside.

The sensitivity to this energy varies in all walks of life. Yes, even the untrained, unconditioned wild ones. Am I positive? Absolutely! Am I negative? Abso-fucking-lutely. Am I balanced? Well, most of the time, I try to be and let it be. I am aware of the fact that some of my language may offend some of you. If it does, this message is not for you.

You can put it down and tell all; please tell all of your loved ones not to read it, if you will. After all, you also, even if you've never been arrested, have the right to remain silent. Or so they say!

"The Sound of Silence," by Simon and Garfunkel, originally has recently been rerecorded by Disturbed and the power of that song is evidence of the awakening of consciousness in humanity. I have always loved music, lyrics, especially. It touches my soul and so I became a song writer, a poet, a singer, and expression of love over hate was and is my desire.

My mission from God is to say, "God is Love." Yes, I went there. With the love of my life. She didn't return to this life in human form. However, her spirit, her love, and her essence is more alive than ever; her spirit, along with the Great Spirits of past, present, and future are here and there, now and then, and within everyone.

You are the creator and the destroyer of your own identity. You are the art and the artist. You are the slave and the master. You are the seen and the unseen.

"And" is not used by humans as much as "or." Have you ever wondered why? Me either. Not until

I was shown life after death. Beyond this dimension, there is more than we can imagine. Within this dimension, we learn to obey and follow the psychopathic leaders, without question.

The brain of the bird controls both sides, the left wing and the right wing. These bird brains own both the left and the right wings and, of course, the body of government. The reason for this analogy is because the symbol of the United States, in my mind, is the American bald eagle, which is a bird of prey. Majestic and beautiful, it was respected and honored by the Native Americans. And then the American Bald Ego (white man) has landed to kill and control and conquer the new Promised Land "all in the name of God" and Greed. The Promised Land, boy, did we fuck that up. As I write this, a song by the Eagles comes to mind. "The Last Resort." Listen to it if you will or read the words and see for yourself, if you can identify with our own hidden human Ego Agenda.

She came from Providence, the one in Rhode Island,
Where the old world shadows hang heavy in the air.
She packed her hopes and dreams like a refugee,
Just as her father came across the sea.
She heard about a place people were smiling.
They spoke about the red man's way,
How they loved the land.
And they came from everywhere
To the Great Divide,
Seeking a place to stand
Or a place to hide

EGONOMICS 101

Down in the crowded bars,
Out for a good time,
Can't wait to tell you all
What it's like up there.
And they called it paradise.
I don't know why.
Somebody laid the mountains low
While the town got high.
You can leave it all behind and sail to Lahaina
Just like the missionaries did so many years ago.
They even brought a neon sign: "Jesus is coming."
Brought the white man's burden down, brought the white man's reign.
Then the chilly winds blew down across the desert,
Through the canyons of the coast, to the Malibu,
Where the pretty people play, hungry for power,
To light up their neon way and give them things to do.
Some rich men came and raped the land; nobody caught 'em.
Put up a bunch of ugly boxes, and Jesus, people bought 'em.
And they called it paradise, the place to be.
They watched the hazy sun sinking in the sea.
Who will provide the grand design?
What is yours and what is mine?
'Cause there is no more new frontier;
we have got to make it here.
We satisfy our endless needs
And justify our bloody deeds
In the name of destiny and in the name of God.
And you can see them there on Sunday morning.
Stand up and sing about what it's like up there.
They call it paradise. I don't know why.
You call some place paradise, kiss it goodbye…

The evil ego-system has been ruling the world for a long time. The economy, ecology, geology, biology, you name it; there is an insatiable ego at the top of the evil human food chain. And this exists at all levels of humanity, or should I say, inhumanity.

It's funny and it's painful, it's enough to raise the dead
the frequency of stupid shit, will zombify your head
when you realize, you are one of them,
ain't that life a bitch, my friend,
ain't that life a bitch,
the Jesus people hate you too, ain't this life a bitch, again!

CHAPTER FOUR

THE RETURN OF JESUS? HOW CAN SOMEONE RETURN, THAT HAS NEVER LEFT?

The science of mind control has fascinated me all my life. Reverse psychology, subliminal messages, straight-up bullying, the big bad wolf, the wicked fucking witch of the west, the list goes on and on. Mind manipulation?

It is important to remind you, the reader, that I am writing this from my out-of-body, out-of-mind, and out-of-this-dimensional-time experience. At the time of the near-death experience in 2008, there is no doubt that upon my return, I was born again. I am no more or less a Christian than I was before.

However, the dimension that I experienced took me on a journey beyond space and time. Did I see Jesus? Of course I did. Along with all the Great

Spirits of past, present, and future. Even the not-so-great souls or spirits were there and here at the exact same time. Imagine that for a moment. Now look around you.

Do you feel the battling force of energy within you and around you? The positive and negative energy is constant. Accept it. The only control you have is to take the apparent negative and turn it or transform it in to positive energy, love the game.

Now, try to be honest with yourself. That is easy for me to say, but I have no desire to make you do it. I am not here to confront, compete, or challenge anybody or anything in this dimension. In my own honesty, even though I'm almost broken down to nothing in the bank and a very diminished ego, my spirit and soul will remain loved by me. Even if you hate it. So love me or hate me, it makes no difference to me.

My soul and I. I could care less. I am positive about my personal negatives. If you ask me what makes me mad or crazy, I would have to say, honestly, nothing and everything at this very moment. The facts and the fallacies of life and death. To be specific in this moment, I am aware of my own illusions and disillusions, as well as yours and theirs. And that is not to judge, just to observe.

Knowledge and Wisdom

Knowledge and wisdom in this reality or on this earth, so to speak, are two entirely different things. Knowing this now grants me peace of mind. In other words, I can't teach fear, if I have very little or none. Knowledge is power! We all know that right?

The forbidden fruit of knowledge, WTF is that? And why was I forced to go to school for twelve years? And then send my children to school. To be programmed. To learn how to be a productive and a reproductive player of this game of life. "The Test" is a song I wrote around 1997 or 1998. This was also the beginning of the Smile 'N' Fish Band, which I helped to create.

"The Test," album Bite Me, by Smile 'N' Fish
Testing, One, Two, Testing…
each and every fuckin' one of you.
Life is a test…It's only a test…
Everybody you know takes the test…
Everybody you know is the test

Other songs:
"Find the Words"
"Birth Garden #9"
"For Alicea"
"Prison of Love"
"This Time"
"Why Do I"
"My Fantasy"

After the accident in 2008, I was fifty years old at the time. I was born December 24, 1957, and the accident was July 20, 2008. I was fifty years, seven months, and twenty-seven days. So born in '57, died and born again at 50.7 or so.

I don't know exactly why I wrote that. I went and took a shower and it came to me. Time travel or going to another dimension, astral projection, elevating consciousness, mental telepathy. All of these are over my head; I can't explain them because I didn't study them.

However, now at this stage of the game, I realize that I have been resonating with this higher self or operating from my soul, more or less, all along. In other words, I was totally unaware of my own invisible ego (lower self), soul (higher self), and the visible me (the center of attraction) or rather, distraction.

People around the world are becoming aware and awakened to what I'm calling the ego-system, that is to say, pseudo-gods or god-like entities that exist in every person alive from the top to the bottom. Yes, even me. My inferior ego hates to be exposed, while at the same moment, my soul is searching for the spotlight at the top of the world, so to speak.

When the top and the bottom and the left and the right come together, then the circle of life is complete. From the next dimension, remember now my soul-self was witnessing the death of my ego, or my lower-self, and it was painless, fearless, and essentially heaven.

EGONOMICS 101

So why in the world would I want to come back to this hell and be reunited with my ego? Because this is heaven and this is hell. As above, so below. It all depends on your perspective and your beliefs. Every word you hear in life goes through your ears and into your brain and either resonates or distorts your frequency.

Your harmonic balance depends on a peaceful mind. And this is not only words; this applies to all five of the common senses at heightened awareness times when all five normal senses are activated on high alert. That is when the sixth sense and maybe even more come into play.

From the normal physical world which is ruled by the collective egos of all of us, we tend to call that dementia or demented or even demonic. In other words, that poor SOB has lost his fuckin' mind. He is seeing things that we can't see and hearing things that we can't hear and so on. So we, the ego- system, must kill him. Silence him before he starts to expose our egos and the back room deals we've got going on.

Look at him trying to be honest in a world of lies. What the fuck? And so it is. You may have come into contact or even contracted some of these deals knowingly or even unknowingly, consciously and subconsciously it seems, lies and deceit are expected more than honesty.

This is the reason we are ordered to keep that shit to ourselves. This is our little secret. Don't tell anyone what you saw and know. They will think we are crazy, and the superior ego of this world, you know, the commander and chief, the God Father, the keeper of your own secret thoughts, is your ego.

CHAPTER FIVE

THE HUMAN RACE? WHAT'S THE HURRY?

The human race. What do those three simple words imply? The words have been around for eons. I believe they predate the Bible. And yet we still identify ourselves by race, color, and/or creed.

Are you purebred or a crossbreed? If you ask me that question, I would honestly say, I don't know and I don't care to know. As far as I know, I am a Native American because I was born here in the good old United States of America. We still call it the United States, but it is becoming more and more un-united every day.

It seems somewhere along the way, the soul of this great nation was sold out from under us. Long before I was born, in 1913 when the Federal Reserve (private banking) was allowed to control the US dollar; that was a sellout. This coincides with the creation of the IRS, and it was probably a good idea at the time.

Yet taxation with shady representation is no better than taxation without representation. In my humble opinion, the shadow government is no longer a theory. Hell, just look at the front runners of the presidential race; is that really the best we can do? Every four years, we are faced with the lesser of two evils. Sounds shady to me. And whoever gets in office makes no difference when both sides are run by the same banking cartel. Which, under any name, is too big to fail.

Well, actually, I was born in Texas. And I was transplanted to California in 1969, at the age of eleven or so. The reason for bringing this up is to reiterate something that was taught to me in junior high social studies. We were told, as a matter of fact, that we are 50 percent culture (our environment) and 50 percent genetics (our heritage).

As a kid from a predominantly German Catholic town in conservative Texas, I was trying to adapt to a new environment (culture dish) in Southern California. Talk about culture shock. At least, I had a 50/50 chance of survival. First on the to-do list was to lose the accent and the flat-top hairdo. The accent was easy.

I didn't even notice the change. The hair took a little more effort. I had to get past my mom's clean-cut preprogrammed fear of the hippy movement. The hippies were the protesters of the established system of greed and control. How dare they protest against and question authority? This is the '70s, and we've got a goddamn war going on against our established enemy, communism. Why don't they cut their fuckin' hair and get a real job or, better yet, join the service?

They (the hippies), at the time, were portrayed by the establishment as enemies of the state. The state I'm referring to here is the state of confusion. The state of mind that I for one lived in for the first fifty years of my life. Unbeknownst to me, I learned to analyze my own being. I learned to read and write. Well, not so much on the reading part, until after the accident.

But for the grace of God, I documented my thoughts through songs and poetry. I learned to love rock 'n' roll and especially, the blues. Even though from my young perspective, both the established church and state condemned it as demonic, devil music.

Hell, they were even playing that shit backward to find the evil secret hidden message. WTF? Who would do that, and why? Our turntable only went in one direction, and I was forbidden to touch the record after it began. So in the words of the great John Lennon, "Let it be." God blessed his soul in both life and death. In other words, even though our physical ego bodies never met, his soul and spirit continue to resonate love, peace, and hope. But only to those who are willing to awaken and dream true love.

The point of this chapter, "The Human Race, What's the Hurry?" is to show the faster we live, the faster we die. No matter what the latest polls of scientific studies or even religions, dogma for that matter, tell you, the #1 cause of death is life itself. So live it up! And by all means, enjoy the race.

After all, if you are alive in this world, you qualify. And even after you/we retire from racing, the point is making it fun. And preferably before your final lap around the sun, you can slow down and notice the rush is over. The human race is killing itself by virtue of the greedy ego-system. So let's change the name of the game.

Yes, I am talking about you and me. The richest of the rich and the poorest of the poor. The master and the slave, the givers and the takers, them and us, I could go on and on with no end. But the point is every individual has these opposing forces within.

Creation and evolution are one and the same. The only difference is blind faith and denial of fact. As a matter of fact, fact and fiction are one and the same. That is an oxymoron, you may think or say, so I ask you to not believe my word, don't take my word for it.

Just look around you: are your vices and devices pleasing and comforting or are they distracting and annoying? Now imagine if you will, a hundred or two hundred years ago. What do you suppose you would have thought about then? Of course, they were thinking the unconscionable. A better future. To know all and with a little effort. The World Wide Web.

The ego-system wants to use technology to gain more control over more people, and it does, through secrets and lies. Subliminally, we are ordered to obey and consume. Feed the ego…kill the soul! Or feed the soul to kill the ego. This personal battle exists in every human being.

Ergo, the human race is the human condition. We are trained to train our young to fear the absence of your trainers. Therefore, unconditional love is as rare today as it was two thousand years ago. And conditional hate is as prevalent as it was two thousand years ago. The human conditioners of ego would have it no other way.

The Watchers

The watchers of the human race
Have never left the stands
they came here long ago from space
To wake the souls of Egoic Man

The spirits and/or aliens
Unseen are just like you
So if you fear, what they intend
They are reflecting us, it's true

CHAPTER SIX

Why?

My dear friend, Dr. Vicky Thomas, who graciously typed and spell-checked this book for me, asked me to write another chapter to include why I am writing this book and who it is for.

First and foremost, this work is for me to explain myself. Or rather, to explain the unexplainable consciousness of the soul beyond this physical dimension of life as we know it. To the best of my ability and in laymen's terms because I am one of the many returning spirits or souls from this other dimension.

In order for me to do this, I have to go out of my body to the source of this death-like experience. From this other dimension, I am able to see and understand the human condition. Mainly the condition of positive and negative energy that flows through me is what I am speaking of.

On the positive side or soul, half of me is the unconditional love of life itself. This includes respecting both life and death. If you fear death, which is what the egoist mind is programmed to do, then you ultimately fear life itself.

It is important to remember all positive emotions are all soul-serving and all negative emotions, hate, fear, anger, etc., are serving the ego (lower-self). This is all part of the human condition. What I am trying to say is the programming of the mind begins at an early age.

It is conditioned to follow the leaders of the ego-system or the human condition. Instead, we should be following our intuition of soul (spirit), this is our mission, to know that peace and love has more strength and power than the opposite. The ego condition is to assume the position of victim or prey and feel hopelessness.

Most of us feel or fear the consequence of speaking out against the machine that controls us. Inadvertently, after a few follow-the-leader lessons, we reinforce that belief on our own. Like I said earlier, the programming begins as soon as you are born. Perhaps, even in the womb where you are literally connected to every emotion and thought had by your mother, both positive and negative. Both real and imagined.

This is where it is important to understand emotions and thought. Even if we are presumed to have one or the other. That is simply not true. Every being has a purpose in this human experience or, rather, experiment. The latter, a glimpse from the other dimension.

Please keep in mind that in that state of being, my human ego, or negative- self, did not exist. However, in order to return to this form of existence or this realm of existence, in this body, I am both positive and negative energy. Yes, in order to be human, my soul had to be reunited with the preconditioned ego of humanity.

The only difference between life now and death then is that I am now aware of and consciously participate in this divine experiment. That is to say, I wish to help change the program and the sublime human programming that most of us are unaware of.

As an American white male, one of nine siblings, with three older brothers and three older sisters, then me, and then two younger brothers, my desire was to find balance of myself. Within the family, I had plenty of examples. We were raised Catholic, as was most of the small towns in Texas. As a kid, I learned to respect authority and my elders.

That meant to me, as I got older, learned to respect myself first. I learned to love myself and love the game of life. As a player of this game in my personal universe (my body), I was the team, the coach, the watcher. I had to play all parts, offence and defense, and ultimately, the referee is my conscience. This would have come in handy, to know my own divided self as a lad, and then later as a dad.

(July 20, 2016, eight years ago today.)

What I am referring to when I say, "divided self," is the human condition of constant conflict within and without. This is regardless of your status in the system. Microcosmic and macrocosmic, it is still cosmic energy, both positive and negative LIFE energy. Conscious action and thought are presumed to be premeditated, pre-manifested, and prescribed to some degree in the mind.

I bring up micro and macro in reference here to the human body as an individual organism. A biological mechanism, supposedly individually operated. That is simply not so. At all/any points in life, we are all influenced by each other, one way or another. This does not end when you die. Even if you think it does.

However, strong, weak, and/or neutrally connected, you are to the source of life, the Great Spirit, known to me at this stage of my soul's evolution as the power of love for all beings. Not, and I must repeat, NOT the love of power over all.

And finally I'd like to end this chapter of this book, Egonomics 101, with the simple answer to the WHY and WHO this book is for. The message is to bring light to the dark side of humanity. It is to help expose the human ego-system for what it is, NOT what it appears and pretends to be. The leaders of this system cannot save you from you. Only you can prevent self-abuse.

Little White Lies

The little white lies you heard as a child
Are the secrets you keep mile after mile
You bury them deep in the back of your mind
In the dead grey matter, it's a matter of time

The closer you get to the end of your road
Is the time to reveal the dirty deeds you behold?
You may seek for help if you need to go deep
Only you hold the key of the prison you keep

Fooling yourself as a victim of fate
Is the only conviction you must contemplate
If the court is in order, the one in your head
You may lie with the judge at night in your bed

And if you get off on this trial of your dreams
You're bound to repeat the process it seems
The little white lies, they don't go away
They turn into lawyers and leaders today

It is to help awaken the human spirit, into the evolution of consciousness, to help shed light on the fact that every child knows that love is stronger than hate. So don't be a hater, don't be a bully, not even to yourself. It is important to try to see yourself in any situation from above yourself, from outside yourself.

Be true to yourself. There is no need to compete for love when you are the love that you are looking for. Yes, you are a co-creator of your world, your life, your being. So we can stop blaming the system of perpetual fear, break it down, and rebuild it. We must begin with truth, regardless of how terrifying it may be to the doctrines of any religion and or government body.

The disclosure project with Dr. Steven Greer is gaining momentum, if you don't know about it, you can Google it. The UFO phenomena can't be hidden forever. Believe it or not, we are not alone! And I am sorry to say, we are not the smartest beings God created.

Your soul/spirit guides can only help you if you intend to help yourself to love. If you love to hate or hate to love, you may need to check your class.

If you have no class, on Capitol Hill
You may want to check, your prescription bill
Obamacare can't relieve your pain
If the pain in your ass is capital gain
To believe big pharmacies, don't push drugs
With side effects, swept under the rug.

The business of Government is out of control
And nobody noticed, the cost of her soul
If Justus is blind, to the lies at the top
Who feed off the bottom, corruption won't stop
To turn a blind eye, to corporate greed
Lady Liberty's ill, her bleeding hearts bleed
So Goddamn the pushers of illicit drugs
And Goddamn the Government's corporate thugs
Goddamn the grand wizards, on Capitol Hill
And God bless the children, who die of free will.

To my son, rest in peace, Raymond

In my life, I have been receiving this message all along; most often in times of solitude, when I'm alone (or in spirit), I am inspired to share this message of love. I am somewhat shy by nature. Therefore, most of the messages gifted to me are songs unsung. However, I will share "My Fantasy" with the hope that it resonates with your soul also.

My Fantasy (1997) Tommy Laux

I have no enemies, at least none that I know.
Everyone helps me, whether friend or foe.
I visit my fantasy, in my fantasy land.
Where we all help each other, whenever we can.
It's the meaning of peace, with a piece for us all.
If I have what you need, would you give me a call?
May I show you the way I found heaven on earth.
By living each day, for all of its worth
By placing my faith in no one living thing.
In my fantasy land, no one man is king.
We all have a heart, and all share one goal.
We all give our best, as it comes from the soul.
Please have no fear, that you don't see what I see.
After all, this is only my own fantasy.

CHAPTER SEVEN

DREAMS

Coincidentally, as I was preparing to send this transcript to my author coach, I ran into Dr. Vicky Thomas, DCH. She brought to my attention some earlier work she and I had done, relating to dreams. I did not know where to put it, so here it is.

After the accident, I realized in all the years of my writing, I go deep when I write or meditate. My therapy has always been early morning, mostly, before I'm fully awake, I pick up a pen and write, I don't have an agenda. Whatever comes through me.

I didn't realize that not everybody does this. I was completely oblivious to that. I assumed everybody did this until I started realizing that I had to learn how to talk to people all over again because of the new depth I go to. This depth is what people shy away from. They are afraid to hear it or they are afraid to stir up the emotions that they have. I have heard those things.

Part of the protective ego that I have noticed in the past that was keeping me quiet is that I tend to pay attention more to shit that's happened around me. Not always the shit that other people wanted me to pay attention to, but I was taking more mental notes than you could even imagine. It's not literally with a pen and paper, it's the self-evaluation process of life.

I tend to date almost everything. I literally have a record of my thought patterns for the last thirty-five years or more. Since I was twenty years old, in 1977, I started writing songs and poetry.

After the accident, I had some friends helping me clean out the garage and found a briefcase with all of those writings in it. And one of the things that was written back then, I remember writing it, but I don't know where it came from. That's where most of my writing comes from, I'm just the medium. I just hold the pen and let it flow through me. It was a full page, front and back, titled "To Suffer Death but Could Not Die."

TOMMY JOE LAUX

To Suffer Death but Could Not Die

All at once things seemed so small,
My breath came short and scarce at all.
But sure the sky is big I said,
Miles and miles above my head.
So here upon my back I lie,
And look my fill unto the sky.
And so I looked and after all,
The sky was not so very tall.
The sky I said must somewhere stop.
And sure enough, I see the top.
The sky I said is not so grand
Almost could touch it with my hand
And reaching up my hand to try,
I screamed to feel it touch the sky.
Something whispered to me a sound,
That deafened the air for worlds around
The cracking of the tinted sky
The ticking of eternity
A thousand people crawl, I died
With each and mourned for all!
A man was staring in capris
He moved his eyes and looked at me.
I felt his gaze, I heard his moan,
And knew his hunger as my own.
I saw at sea a great fog bank,
Between two ships that struck and sank.
A thousand screams came from the boat
And every scream tore through my throat
I had no pain, I felt no death

What I felt was each last breath.
And so beneath the weight I lie…
And suffered death but could not die.
Deep in the earth, I rested now,
I got here, but I know not how.
Then the rain began to fall,
It sounded friendly after all.
For rain had such a friendly sound,
To one who's six feet underground.
Scarce is a friendly voice or face,
A grave is such a lonely place.
How can I bear it buried here?
While overhead, the sky grows clear.
Oh please I said, give me new birth,
And set me back upon the earth.
There was a crash, a vicious rage.
The rain had washed me from my grave.
I know not how such things can be,
I only know they came to me,
I breathe my soul back into me.
Up from the ground again sprang I
And hailed the earth with such a cry,
Has not been heard by any man
Who have been dead and lives again!

    This is what happened to him! Tommy wrote that poem thirty years prior to his accident. I believe some have better filters, I've heard of these filters. To me, after the accident, the filters that were formed in my brain for over fifty years were rattled loose. You could call it filters or calcification or a numbing effect that keeps that third eye blind or foggy and keeps it from being activated. That was knocked loose in mine. It opened up so much of my mind. It wasn't completely shut off before because I've had these gifts of imagination all of my life, that's where that part comes from, but a lot of what I'm aware of now is that I no longer have to filter my imagination out. The word imagination in this context may be misleading because what I am referring to here is intuition of things to come. Not necessarily controlled by my intellectual masculine mind. It is more like it came from a feminine spirit of intuition.

At a young age where you've had this overabundance of artistic imagination, a dreamer if you will, you're labeled. You're not conforming, and that happened at a very young age. I failed the first grade because they called me a daydreamer. At this stage, I've pretty much got it perfected. I don't just wait to go to sleep to dream, I'm doing it all the time.

But after the accident, in that time frame, I could look back in my writings and see what the thoughts were. Ultimately, what that comes to is, communication. I was noticing that I had to learn how to talk all over again because I lost my female voice, she died. And she's kind of speaking through me, so I had to try to understand that mechanism, that side of the brain, or that heart.

I had to think with that part of the heart. That was completely new to me. I didn't know that you could think with your heart. I knew a little bit about it, but I became more aware of the need for that element. Now I am able to go inside myself and I see the mechanisms, I see the switches, I see everything; I go inside my brain, inside my heart, and inside it is vast, it is its own universe.

The accident was July 20, and around December, with the coaching of friends and family, they told me I needed to go see a grief counselor. I decided to go ahead and do that so I made an appointment. That morning, I woke up and started writing like I do every morning.

Dream?

The last thing I remember,
we were flying down the road
A flash of light and thunder
Heaven is to be unsold
We floated to the pearly gates
Together hand in hand,
one of us was welcome there,
the other back to land
I don't know who decided
Which one of us would stay
My hell was intensified
I had more dues to pay
My love has encouraged me
To go back and be strong
Life is just a flash in time
We'll be together 'fore too long
The last thing I remember of that fateful day
Is the fact you gotta love each and every day

I had written that that morning, and that afternoon, I went to the grief counselor, and she asked me, "Do you dream?"

"Yea, I dream, doesn't everybody?"

"But do you dream about the accident?"

"No, I don't remember the accident."

"Do you dream about Julie?"

"I don't know if I dream about her, but she's here right now, if you call that a dream, then I am dreaming right now."

It was kind of a conversation where I didn't know how to answer. I had totally forgotten about the writing I did that morning. When I got home and saw what I wrote that morning, I titled it "Dream?" with a question mark because I wrote it as a memory, not as a dream. In depth, there is very little separation between dreams and reality, but

Society doesn't want that, you know, that's not a part of the real world, so they say.

Dr. Vicky's thoughts:

Dreams are very important. They are messages from the unconscious mind. This is true of day dreams and night dreams. The problem is people, even many professionals, have no true idea of how to interpret them. People have an odd dream, go to the bookstore, and pick up a dream book and look up some topic they think relates to the dream, and walk away, thinking, "Well, that's odd," or "Wow!

I'm gonna make a lot of money!" or some such idea, but dream books are only archetypical.

By this I mean, they may take a simple noun and say it means something, but it only really means that to the author! Sure, there are symbols that mean similar things to many people, but this is exactly what Tommy means when he says we have filters or programs that come from society and other people.

Let me give you an example:

My husband and I were walking through Barnes and Noble, and there was a big, beautiful dream book there on a table. It was beautiful. It was artistic. It drew me in! So I picked it up and looked up a recurring theme from my childhood dreams: Horses. It said, "Horse dreams mean you are loving your freedom." It even had meanings for black, brown, or colored horses…this just didn't agree with my interpretation.

As a child, I grew up with a brother who raised horses (and still does.) They are a lot of work. I've been kicked in the belly, thrown off in the middle of a road, taken on a wild, crazy, uncontrolled ride, and knocked off by a horse that knew exactly where every low tree branch existed, bitten, and squished by horses.

To me, they are overgrown dogs and less well behaved. So I asked Jim what he thought deep down inside about horses. His answer, "Big, sweet, eating and shitting machine, total sucking of money down the manure pile." Well, it was pretty clear that a horse only meant freedom to someone else!

So I dug a little deeper into that proverbial pile of manure and I created a couple of ways to interpret YOUR dreams.

First, and most importantly, is to keep a record of your dreams. Keep a notebook or journal by your bed to write them down as soon as you remember them because even a few minutes can make them fuzzy. The first way to interpret is easiest. Everyone in your dream is you. So jot down every character and what they are doing and how they are feeling. Each character is a part of you that you need to pay attention to.

My favorite example of this was a young mother who came to see me and was stressed about a dream. It went like this: We'll call her A. In her dream, A. was making out with her new boyfriend (the first since her divorce over a year before.) In the dream, her ex-husband came along, grabbed her, and pulled her through the car window. He started beating her up while her boyfriend just watched.

When I explained "Everyone in your dream is you," she understood instantly. "I'm beating myself up for having feelings about someone, and I'm just letting myself do it!" For her, that was profound. We followed up with a hypnosis session that allowed her to explore a new relationship carefully and at the pace that was exactly right for her.

The second way to interpret is more complex, but often gives much deeper insights to your dreams than you could ever imagine.

Here's an example of a recent dream I had: I was standing in an open grassy area surrounded by woods. Right in front of me was a fence, which was keeping me from moving onto the grassy area. There was a person, a friend (but I don't recognize who), standing right beside me. The day was sunny and warm.

Suddenly, I saw a beautiful rainbow lorikeet flying above and toward us. I said, "Watch out, he's going to poop on us!"

And sure enough, he pooped, but it was far from us. Then I knew I could hold my arm up and he would land on my arm. So I held my arm up and he landed on it. I was able to pet him, and he was a sweet bird.

The first step is to write down every significant element of your dream. Take your time. Write down people, places, things, and feelings that are important. Make a very complete list down one side of the paper. The second step (and so important) is to now forget about the dream! This allows you to dissociate from the dream. On a separate page, focus on the elements of the dream.

Here are the elements of this dream:

1. The open grassy area
2. Surrounding woods
3. A fence (impeding my movement)
4. An unspecific friend
5. A sunny warm day
6. A rainbow lorikeet
7. Bird poop, getting pooped on at a safe distance
8. The knowledge of control of behavior
9. The feeling of caring for something and its appreciation

(As you can begin to see, this dream is specifically mine! These archetypes only mean things to me specifically!)

Step three is on yet another page. This creates now, a Double Dissociation from the dream. Ask yourself, "What does each element mean to me?"

Here are the meanings of these elements to me.

A. Calmness
B. Unknown areas
C. A block to moving forward
D. Someone else is involved, but I don't know who
E. Something helpless at first, then grows up (I raised them for about ten years)
F. Sometimes things you help poop on you!
G. Sometimes they don't!
H. I can help retrain people and animals
I. I can help people control their behavior

J. I care for people and animals and love their appreciation

Step four is to recognize six areas of life we can change and then apply the meanings to these areas of life. Now ask yourself, what does this mean to me in terms of the following:

1. Relationships/family
2. Health and fitness
3. Personal growth
4. Spiritual growth
5. Career
6. Finances

If I were to take those meanings and apply to relationships, the meaning of the dream would be:

Stay calm when you enter unknown areas of your family and your relationships. There will be unknown areas. Stay calm and observe your own blocks. You do have friends who will be involved, but they remain unknown right now. As people and animals grow up, they are on their own journey and sometimes will poop on you! But remember, sometimes, they won't. You have the ability to help others.

CONCLUSION

This book is an attempt to help anyone who has a problem with addiction of any kind. Not just the obvious ones like drugs and alcohol. What I am referring to is any and all disorders. There are too many to list here.

Wikipedia's definition: Addiction is a medical condition characterized by compulsive engagement in rewarding stimuli, despite adverse consequences.

As I write this, on August 25, 2016, we are in another presidential election year. I will start at the top of human addiction. This is the addiction to POWER. At any level of life, if the power granted to you is abused and/or misused, it is dark energy. This includes hidden agendas, fear tactics, and deceit of any kind.

We all know that politicians and lawyers have a knack for spinning the truth into lies, or lies into truth, to make them believable to themselves if no one else. Any way you spin it, it is still a lie. The lesser of two evil doers is all we are ever presented with. I am by no means perfect because I, too, have evolved with the social disorders of society.

However, I no longer have the desire to lie or believe in the spin, as it is distorted and then presented. I do believe in the Great Spirit. However, the once great nation that I was born into, the United States of America, not so much at this time, because she has sold her soul to the New World Order.

Printed in the USA
CPSIA information can be obtained
at www.ICGtesting.com
LVHW070913060424
776632LV00001B/7